# MORE PRAISE FOR BABYMOUSE!

"Sassy, smart . . .
Babymouse is here
to stay."
**—The Horn Book Magazine**

"Young readers
will happily
fall in line."
**—Kirkus Reviews**

"The brother-sister creative team hits the mark
with humor, sweetness, and characters so genuine
they can pass for real kids." **—Booklist**

"Babymouse is spunky, ambitious,
and, at times, a total dweeb."
**—School Library Journal**

# Be sure to read all the **BABYMOUSE** books:

# CAMP BABYMOUSE

BY JENNIFER L. HOLM & MATTHEW HOLM

RANDOM HOUSE NEW YORK

HEY! I'M **NOT** A WORK OF FICTION!

Copyright © 2007 by Jennifer Holm and Matthew Holm. All rights reserved. Published in the United States by Random House Children's Books, a division of Random House, Inc., New York.

www.randomhouse.com/kids
www.babymouse.com

Educators and librarians, for a variety of teaching tools, visit us at
www.randomhouse.com/teachers

Library of Congress Cataloging-in-Publication Data
Holm, Jennifer L.
Babymouse : Camp Babymouse / Jennifer L. Holm and Matthew Holm.
   p.   cm.
ISBN: 978-0-375-83988-7 (trade) — ISBN: 978-0-375-93988-4 (lib. bdg.)
1. Graphic novels.  I. Holm, Matthew.  II. Title.  III. Title: Camp Babymouse.
PN6727.H592B26 2007   741.5—dc22   2006050391

MANUFACTURED IN MALAYSIA   10  9  8  7  6

RANDOM HOUSE and colophon are registered trademarks of Random House, Inc.

THE WILDERNESS.

THE MOST SAVAGE PLACE ON EARTH.

THEY'LL NEVER FIND US!
SHIVER
SHIVER
WE'LL DIE COLD AND ALONE!
SHIVER
I DON'T WANT TO DIE IN THE WILDERNESS! WAAAAHH!!!

WE'RE ALMOST THERE, BABYMOUSE.

ALMOST WHERE, BABYMOUSE?

POP!

SLEEP-AWAY CAMP!

CAMP? YOU AREN'T EXACTLY THE "CAMPING" TYPE, BABYMOUSE.

WHY DO YOU SAY THAT?

DON'T YOU REMEMBER?

SNAKE! SNAKE!

IT'S A GARDEN HOSE, BABYMOUSE.

BABYMOUSE! BABYMOUSE!
CAMP WILD WHISKERS
"WHERE GIRLS GO TO GET LOST!"
YAY

19

BETTER GET A BUNK, BABYMOUSE.

OCCUPIED

NOPE

TAKEN

FORGET IT

SORRY

NO VACANCY

NO WAY

UH-UH

20

23

THAT AFTERNOON.

OOF!

PUT YOUR MUSCLES INTO IT, BABYMOUSE.

UNGH!

TWANG!

EMPTY.

WHERE'D IT GO?

YOU DON'T WANT TO KNOW, BABYMOUSE.

AAAAGGHH!! MESSY WHISKERS!!!

HEY! MY WHISKERS AREN'T THAT MESSY!

43

THAT NIGHT.

CAN'T GET COMFORTABLE!

ROLL

RUSTLE

BE CAREFUL, BABYMOUSE.

FLIP!

WHUMP!

BABYMOUSE. VERY DISAPPOINTING. YOUR CABIN WILL GET TEN DEMERITS.

BABYMOUSE!!!

LATER.

NOW WE WILL OBSERVE BIRDS IN THEIR NATURAL ENVIRONMENT!

UNGH!

OOH!

WHOA!

SLIP!

FLIP!

TWANG!

SQUAWK!

52

SHIVER

SPLASH

SPLASH

SPLASH

SPLASH

COME ON, BABYMOUSE. GET IN THERE OR YOUR CABIN WILL GET A DEMERIT.

SHE HAD SEARCHED FAR AND WIDE FOR THE FAMED CREATURE...

SPOUT!

THE WHITE WHALE!

CAPTAIN BABYMOUSE WOULD NOT FAIL.

GRR

GOT YOU NOW!

SWISH!

SPOUT!

THUNK!

ROAR!

THAT NIGHT.

BRUSH

BRUSH

LATRINE

TRUDGE TRUDGE TRUDGE

BABYMOUSE IS RUINING EVERYTHING FOR US!

the Buttercup

70

We're not home right now. Leave a message at the beep. *BEEP!*
PHONE
PHONE

MOM! DAD! I WANT TO COME HOME! I MISS YOU! I'M HAVING A TERRIBLE TIME! PLEASE COME GET ME AND—

*BEEP!* No room left on tape!

TYPICAL.

73

75

! 

:WINK:

STUPID
FLASHLIGHT
BATTERIES.

BANG
SHAKE

DIDN'T YOU
PACK EXTR
BATTERIES
BABYMOUSE

SURE-
IN MY
TRUN

PARKING LOT

NORTH WOODS

CROOKED TREE

LATRINE

START HERE

BIG ROCK

WATERFALL

BONFIRE CIRCLE

PAY PHONE

C

MESS HALL

DOCK

CABIN 7

LAKE

BEACH

AT BREAKFAST.

IT WAS SO SCARY! I NEVER WOULD HAVE MADE IT BACK WITHOUT BABYMOUSE!

WAY TO GO, BABYMOUSE!

LISTEN UP, CAMPERS! THE FINAL COMPETITION WILL BE TOMORROW MORNING. IT WILL BE A SCAVENGER HUNT! PICK A TEAM LEADER.

... AND IN LAST PLACE ARE... THE BUTTERCUPS.

CABIN SCOREBOARD
BUSY BEES....... 107
DAFFODILS....... 99
SNAPDRAGONS... 72
FLUFFY BUNNIES... 56
SUNFLOWERS.... 48
HONEY BEARS.... 45
BUTTERCUPS.. (-27)

BUT—BUT—BUT WE WON THE SCAVENGER HUNT!

SORRY, BABYMOUSE. ONE WIN WASN'T ENOUGH TO MAKE UP FOR ALL THOSE DEMERITS.

# CAMP WILD WHISKERS MERIT BADGES

SWIMMING

COOKING

FIRST AID

ARCHERY

THERE'S A NEW ICE PRINCESS...

AND SHE'S READY...

TO SKATE INTO YOUR HEART...

# BABYMOUSE  SKATER GIRL!

TWIRL...!!

# COMING IN FALL 2007!

WHIRL!

CAN'T STOP SPINNING!

CLUNK!

TYPICAL. OW.

# BABYMOUSE BONUS!

## • TIPS ON BEING A CAMPER •

  FIRST, PACK YOUR GEAR!

 BACKPACK

 SLEEPING BAG

 BUG SPRAY

  CUPCAKES FOR ENERGY

  NOW HIT THE TRAIL!

COMPASS

OBSERVE.          COLLECT.          RUN!

BEES

POKE

UNGH!

BUZZ!

AAAGH!